824

The Fire Station

Sue Barraclough

Photographs by Chris Fairclough

W
FRANKLIN WATTS
LONDON • SYDNEY

First published in 2006 by
Franklin Watts
338 Euston Road,
London NW1 3BH

Franklin Watts Australia
Level 17/207 Kent Street
Sydney NSW 2000

ISBN: 978 0 7496 6919 5

A CIP catalogue record for this book is available
from the British Library.
Dewey Decimal Classification: 363.37

Planning and production by Discovery Books Limited
Editors: Paul Humphrey and Sue Barraclough
Designer: Jemima Lumley
Photography: Chris Fairclough

The author, packager and publisher would like to thank Avon Fire and
Rescue Service for their help and participation in this book. The DVD shown
on page 27 was produced by Leicestershire Fire and Rescue Service.

Printed in Malaysia

Franklin Watts is a division of Hachette Children's Books,
an Hachette Livre UK company
www.hachettelivre.co.uk

Contents

The fire station

A fire station is where firefighters wait on **standby** to go out to fight fires or carry out rescues. Behind the fire station is a big **drill** yard to practise skills.

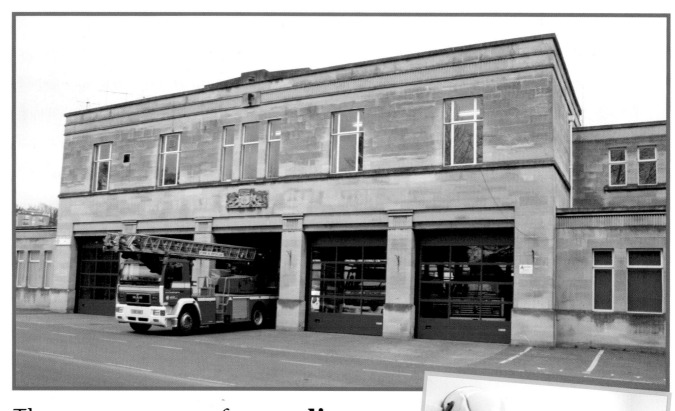

There are garages for **appliances** (fire engines) and storerooms for fire and rescue **equipment**. Fire and rescue uniforms are kept in one room so firefighters can put them on quickly when the alarm sounds.

There is a **watch** of firefighters on duty day and night.
This is White Watch. The watch is divided up so there
is a **crew** for each appliance.

Part of the fire
station is a fire
safety centre. This is
where teams of
officers work with
schools and families
teaching fire safety.

The team

The fire station team is made up of firefighters, fire safety officers and **support staff**. They work together to respond to **emergency** calls and teach fire safety and **prevention**.

Alison and Mary work in the **reception**. They greet visitors to the fire safety centre.

Preventing fires and keeping safe

In the fire safety centre, officers set up activities for groups of children to help them learn.

Firefighter AVI is an information point in the fire safety centre. It has games to help people learn about keeping safe and fire prevention.

Firefighters also visit homes to give advice about keeping safe and to fit smoke alarms.

Some officers work in the **arson task force** (see pages 26-27). They work mainly with schools.

Starting work

At the start of a watch, there is a team meeting to talk about **duties** and jobs.

The equipment is checked at the start of a watch, and after every **call-out**. Most equipment for fighting fires and for rescues is stored in the appliances.

All vehicles are checked too. This safety boat is used at fires and rescues near water. The crew check that everything is working, and that all the equipment is in the right place.

'Finding a piece of equipment fast can make all the difference during a rescue.'
Steve, firefighter

Fire control

When someone makes a 999 call it goes to the **fire control centre**. The centre is open day and night.

The controllers have maps and information to help them work out where to send a fire crew. Then they send all the details through to the fire station that is closest.

Vehicles and equipment

The appliance carries all the fire and rescue equipment needed to put out a fire or rescue people.

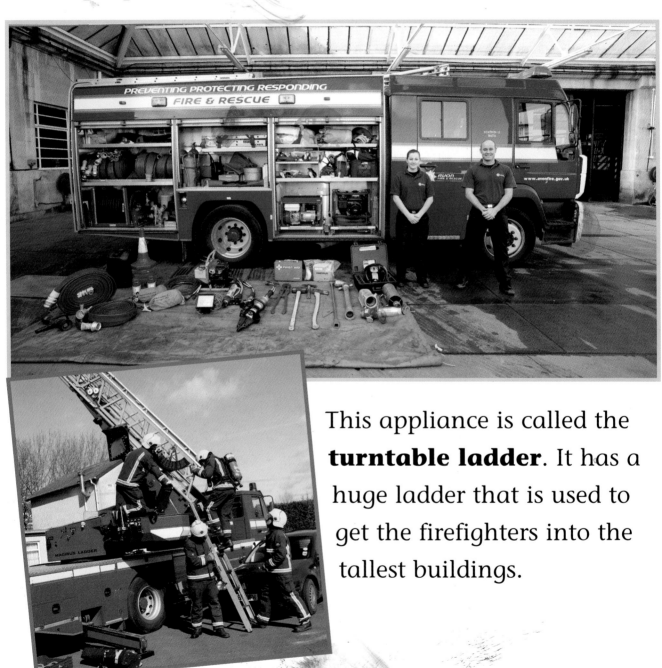

This appliance is called the **turntable ladder**. It has a huge ladder that is used to get the firefighters into the tallest buildings.

Each firefighter wears a uniform that is designed to protect him or her from head to toe. A helmet and **visor** protect the head and face, and strong boots protect the feet.

Firefighters also wear strong gloves to protect their hands while they are working.

The safety boat is pulled to the water by a pick-up truck. Here, the crew carry out a rescue in the water.

Fire drill

Firefighters do drills to practise their skills. Here, they practise arriving at a fire. Jamie is the fire incident commander. His white helmet shows he is in charge.

As soon as they have their orders, the crew start to unload the equipment that they need.

Steve opens the **fire hydrant**. The hoses are unrolled and attached.

Jamie stands back to make sure that everyone is working safely, and that they know what to do.

Incident commander

At a fire it is important that one person is in charge. Fire incident commanders do not fight fires. They stand back to watch what is happening and decide how best to fight a fire.

Fire and rescue

Now, the firefighters practise a rescue using the fire station practice tower.

They pretend that someone is trapped by a fire. First, the ladders are moved into place.

Mark turns on the tap, and the building is blasted with water to bring the fire under control.

Once the fire is under control, the firefighters can get into the building.

The rescue team practise lowering a **casualty** down to the ground on a **stretcher**.

Breathing apparatus

Firefighters often need to put on **breathing apparatus**. The smoke from a fire makes it difficult to breathe. These firefighters put on their apparatus fast but carefully.

A mask covers the face so there is air to breathe.

Part of the kit is a unit that beeps loudly if a firefighter does not move for some time. This makes sure the rest of the team know there is a problem.

Darren (below) is the entry control officer. This means it is his job to keep a record of who goes into the building.

He also keeps in touch with the firefighters by radio.

Keeping safe

Darren has a board to keep a record of all the firefighters. He knows where they are at all times.

'Fires can kill, so we must make sure that firefighters have back-up to keep them safe.'

Darren, firefighter

Road accidents

Firefighters are also called out to help with road accidents. They have special equipment for cutting metal and glass. They use this cutting equipment to get people safely out of vehicles that have been damaged in a **collision**.

Old cars are kept in the fire station drill yard. The watch use these cars to practise using the cutting equipment.

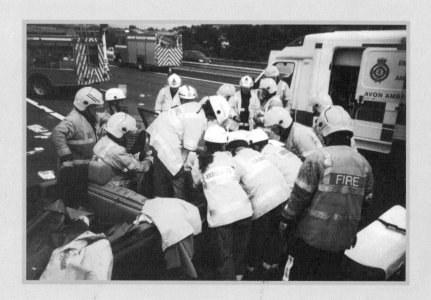

After the drill, all the equipment is put away in the right place.

Working as a team

At a road accident firefighters often need to work closely with **paramedics** and the police to rescue injured people.

Emergency call-out

When a 999 call is made, the controller works out which fire station is nearest and sends a message. Now the firefighters can put the skills they have practised to the test.

At the fire station, the message comes through on the **printer**.

Firefighters leave their boots and trousers together so they are easy to pull on fast when the alarm sounds.

The crew climb into the appliance and set off fast. The lights flash and the siren blares to warn people they are on their way to an emergency.

The firefighters work together to stop the fire. A fire needs to be put out quickly before it spreads.

Keeping fit and healthy

Firefighters need to be fit and strong. The fire station has a gym next to the garage. Firefighters lift weights and use other equipment to keep fit.

'Regular equipment checks, drills and exercise mean we are always ready for any emergency.'
Billy, firefighter

Lifting and carrying

Firefighters need to be fit and healthy, because a big part of the job is lifting and carrying heavy equipment.

Above the garage there is a canteen. There is plenty of room for the whole watch to sit and eat their meals.

Jane works in the canteen kitchen. She cooks food and prepares meals that can be ready later in the day when she is not on duty. If the watch come in late at night after a call-out they can quickly prepare a meal.

There is also space for the firefighters to play pool and table tennis.

Home fire safety visit

Crews visit people's homes to give advice on fire safety and to fit smoke alarms. The whole crew goes in the appliance in case there is an emergency call while they are out.

The crew unload the ladders and tools that they need to fit the smoke alarms.

Mark talks with Catherine about fire safety. Everyone should have a plan so they know what to do if there is a fire in their home.

The firefighters fit the smoke alarm in the hallway. This smoke alarm will bleep loudly if there is a fire.

Fitting smoke alarms

A smoke alarm is cheap and easy to install. Ask an adult to fit one on every floor of your home, and test it often. Choose one with the **British Standard Kitemark**.

Arson task force

Arson is when a fire is started on purpose. Ian and Colin are going to a school to give a **presentation** about arson. They put their equipment into the car.

At the school, Ian talks to the children about the dangers of starting fires.

'Over half of all fires put out by firefighters have been started on purpose.'
Ian, Arson Task Force Officer

Then Colin puts on a DVD where firefighters talk about the dangers of arson. The film shows the serious injuries and burns caused by fires. It shows how quickly a fire can spread and how deadly it can be.

Arson damage

This picture shows the damage arson can cause. People, including firefighters, are sometimes badly burned or killed in these fires.

Finishing work

Towards the end of the watch, Mark makes a note on the board about any equipment that has been damaged or is missing.

A mechanic carries out a service on one of the appliances to make sure it is working well.

As part of the handover to the next watch, Jamie (above, left) talks about ordering new equipment with the officer who is taking over.

Once the handover is complete, White Watch can change out of their work clothes and go home.

Glossary

appliances firefighting vehicles.

arson task force arson is starting a fire on purpose. A task force is a group that is set up to try to stop something happening.

breathing apparatus equipment that helps you breathe.

British Standard Kitemark a symbol that shows something has been made well.

call-out a message or alarm that calls for help.

casualty someone who is hurt.

collision when two or more objects crash together.

crew people needed to work an emergency vehicle.

drill doing tasks or activities to practise something.

duties the things you do as part of your job.

emergency something that needs urgent action.

equipment things you need to do a task.

fire control centre a place where 999 calls are answered and passed to the best team to respond.

fire hydrant a tap in the street where firefighters can fix their hoses to get water to fight a fire.

paramedics people who are trained to give emergency medical help.

presentation a talk to a group of people usually with pictures and diagrams.

prevention to take action to stop something happening.

printer a machine that receives typed messages.

reception a place in a building to welcome visitors.

standby to be ready for action.

stretcher a frame covered with material for carrying ill or injured people.

support staff workers who do paperwork and other office tasks.

turntable ladder a ladder that is attached to a metal turntable that turns the ladder in the right direction.

visor a strong piece of plastic to protect the face.

watch a team of firefighters on duty together.

Further information

Websites
www.avonfire.gov.uk The fire station in this book is part of Avon Fire and Rescue. Visit this site to find out more.

www.fireservice.co.uk This website gives information about the different fire services across the UK, so you can find out about your local fire service.

www.firekills.gov.uk This is a useful site for fire safety information.

Books
Firefighters (People Who Help Us series), Clare Oliver, Franklin Watts, 2002

Firefighter (When I'm At Work series), Sue Barraclough, Franklin Watts, 2005

Every effort has been made by the Packagers and Publishers to ensure that these websites contain no inappropriate or offensive material. However, because of the nature of the Internet, it is impossible to guarantee that the contents of these sites will not be altered. We strongly advise that Internet access is supervised by a responsible adult.

Index